MRS BEE[TON]

A GREAT TRA[DITION]
· SINCE 1[861]

FAVOURITE
RECIPES

© Ward Lock 1985

All Rights reserved.

Produced specially for Damart
by Ward Lock Ltd, 82 Gower Street, London WC1E 6EQ.

Text filmset in Plantin
by Paul Hicks Limited
Burrington Way, Plymouth.

Printed in Belgium
ISBN 0 7063 4269 0

ACKNOWLEDGEMENTS

The publishers would like to thank the following organizations
and companies for their help with the photographs in this book:

Anchor Foods Limited; British Sausage Bureau;
Colmans of Norwich; Eggs Information Bureau;
Guernsey Tomato Information Bureau;
Mushroom Growers Association;
National Dairy Council; Potato Marketing Board;
RHM Foods Ltd; Seafish Industry Authority;
Tate and Lyle Refineries.

PREVIOUS PAGES:
Left: Sponge Pudding (page 33)
Right: Liver and Potato Casserole (page 21)

CONTENTS

Soups

HOTCH POTCH

Serves 8

900g/2 lb scrag and middle neck of lamb *or* mutton
1.5 litres/2½ pints water
1 × 10ml spoon/1 dessertspoon salt
bouquet garni
1 medium-sized carrot, diced
1 small turnip, diced
6 spring onions, cut into thin rings

1 small lettuce, shredded
100g/4 oz shelled young broad beans *or* runner beans, shredded
100g/4 oz cauliflower florets
175g/6 oz shelled peas
salt and pepper
1 × 15ml spoon/1 tablespoon chopped parsley

Remove the meat from the bone and cut the meat into small pieces. Put the bone and meat into a large saucepan, add the water, and heat very slowly to simmering point. Add the salt and the bouquet garni, cover and simmer very gently for 30 minutes. Add the carrot, turnip and spring onions to the pan, cover and simmer for 1½ hours. Add the rest of the vegetables, cover and simmer for a further 30 minutes, then season to taste. Skim off the fat and remove the bouquet garni and the bones. Add the chopped parsley just before serving.

CREAM OF MUSHROOM SOUP

Serves 4

300ml/½ pint white stock
  (see page 8)
225g/8 oz mushroom stalks *or*
  large mushrooms, chopped
1 medium-sized onion,
  chopped
25g/1 oz butter *or* margarine
25g/1 oz flour

600ml/1 pint milk
salt and pepper
150ml/¼ pint single cream
1 egg yolk

GARNISH
chopped parsley

Heat the stock to boiling point in a large saucepan and add the vegetables, reserving a few mushroom pieces for garnish. Cover, and cook until the vegetables are tender, then purée them.

Melt the fat in the cleaned saucepan, add the flour, and stir over gentle heat for 2 – 3 minutes without allowing it to colour. Gradually add the milk, stirring well. Heat to boiling point and simmer for 2 – 3 minutes, stirring constantly. Stir in the vegetable purée, re-heat to boiling point, and season to taste. Cool slightly, then add the reserved mushroom pieces. Add a little of the soup to the cream and yolk, and beat well. Whisk the mixture into the rest of the soup and re-heat gently, stirring all the time. Garnish the finished soup with chopped parsley.

BASIC STOCK

Makes 1.2 litres/2 pints (approx)

900g/ 2 lb cooked or raw bones of any meat or poultry, chopped into manageable pieces *or* cooked or raw meat trimmings, giblets and bacon rinds

salt

450g/1 lb onions, carrots, celery and leeks, sliced

1 bay leaf

4 black peppercorns

Put the bones into a saucepan, cover with cold water and add 1 × 2.5ml spoon/½ teaspoon salt for each 1.2 litres/2 pints of water used. Heat slowly to simmering point. Add the other ingredients, and simmer, uncovered, for at least 3 hours.

Strain the stock and cool quickly by standing the pan in chilled water. When cold, skim off the fat. If the stock is not required at once, keep it cold. Use within 24 hours, or within 3 days if kept in a refrigerator. Reboil before use.

WHITE STOCK

Makes 2.4 litres/4 pints (approx)

900g/2 lb knuckle of veal, chopped into manageable pieces

2.4 litres/4 pints cold water

1 × 10ml spoon/1 dessertspoon salt

1 × 10ml spoon/1 dessertspoon white vinegar *or* lemon juice

1 medium-sized onion, sliced

1 stick of celery, sliced

1 × 2.5ml spoon/½ teaspoon white peppercorns

a small strip of lemon rind

1 bay leaf

Put the bones in a large pan with the cold water, salt and vinegar or lemon juice. Heat to boiling point and skim. Add the vegetables and the other ingredients. Bring back to the boil, cover, reduce the heat, and simmer gently for 4 hours.

Strain the stock through a fine sieve and cool it quickly by standing the pan in chilled water. When cold, skim off the fat. Use within 24 hours, or within 3 days if kept in a refrigerator. Reboil before use. Use as required.

CREAM OF CHICKEN SOUP

Serves 4 – 6

25g/1 oz cornflour
150ml/¼ pint milk
1.2 litres/2 pints chicken stock
50g/2 oz cooked chicken, diced
salt and pepper
1 × 5ml spoon/1 teaspoon
  lemon juice

a pinch of grated nutmeg
2 egg yolks
2 × 15ml spoons/2 tablespoons
  single cream

Blend the cornflour with a little of the milk. Heat the stock to boiling point and stir into the blended cornflour. Return the mixture to the pan and re-heat to boiling point, stirring all the time. Reduce the heat, cover and simmer for 20 minutes. Add the chicken, and heat in the soup. Season to taste, and add the lemon juice and nutmeg. Beat the yolks with the rest of the milk and the cream, then beat in a little hot soup, and fold into the rest of the soup. Heat until it thickens, but do not allow it to boil.

BROWN ONION SOUP

Serves 6

25g/1 oz butter *or* margarine
3 large Spanish onions,
  chopped
1.2 litres/2 pints stock
bouquet garni
salt and pepper

2 × 10ml spoons/
  2 dessertspoons flour for
  each 600ml/1 pint puréed
  soup
cold stock, water *or* milk

Melt the fat in a large saucepan, add the onions, and fry gently for about 20 minutes until browned. Add the stock, bouquet garni and seasoning to taste. Heat to boiling point, reduce the heat, and simmer gently until the onions are quite soft. Do not overcook. Remove the bouquet garni. Purée the vegetables and liquid. Weigh the flour in the correct proportion and blend it with a little cold stock, water or milk, then stir it into the soup. Bring to the boil, stirring all the time, and cook for 5 minutes. Re-season if required.

CREAM OF TOMATO SOUP

Serves 4

50g/2 oz butter *or* margarine
550g/1¼ lb tomatoes, chopped
1 small onion, chopped
1 medium-sized carrot, chopped
1 stick of celery, sliced
25g/1 oz lean bacon, without rinds and chopped

600ml/1 pint white stock (see page 8)
bouquet garni
salt and pepper
25g/1 oz flour
300ml/½ pint milk
4 × 10ml spoons/ 4 dessertspoons single cream

Melt half the fat in a large saucepan, add the vegetables and bacon, and fry gently for 5 minutes. Add the stock and bouquet garni, and season to taste. Heat to boiling point, and simmer gently until the vegetables are soft. Remove the bouquet garni. Rub through a fine sieve.

Using the rest of the fat, melt it in the cleaned saucepan, add the flour and stir over gentle heat for 2 – 3 minutes without allowing it to colour. Gradually add the milk, stirring well. Heat to boiling point, and simmer for 2 – 3 minutes, stirring constantly. Stir in the vegetable purée, re-heat to boiling point, and season to taste. Cool slightly. Add a little of the soup to the single cream, and beat well. Whisk the mixture into the rest of the soup, and heat gently, stirring all the time.

COCK-A-LEEKIE

Serves 8

100g/4 oz prunes
1 small boiling fowl with
　giblets
900g/2 lb beef marrow bones,
　chopped into manageable
　pieces
3 rashers streaky bacon,
　without rinds, chopped

2 × 5ml spoons/2 teaspoons
　salt
450g/1 lb leeks, cut into thin
　rings
½ × 2.5ml spoon/¼ teaspoon
　pepper
bouquet garni

Soak the prunes overnight in cold water, then stone them. Put the fowl, giblets, marrow bones and bacon into a deep pan, cover with cold water, add the salt and heat very slowly to simmering point. Reserve 4 × 15ml spoons/4 tablespoons of the leeks and add the remaining leeks, the pepper and bouquet garni to the pan. Cover and simmer gently for about 3 hours or until the fowl is tender.

Remove the fowl, carve off the meat and cut it into fairly large serving pieces. Strain the liquid then return the pieces to the soup with the prunes and the remaining leeks. Simmer very gently for 30 minutes until the prunes are just tender but not broken. Re-season if required. Serve the soup with the prunes.

Fish

STUFFED WHOLE PLAICE

Serves 4

4 small plaice
25g/1 oz butter

STUFFING
100g/4 oz mild Cheddar
  cheese, grated
50g/2 oz soft white
  breadcrumbs
1 × 5ml spoon/1 teaspoon dry
  mustard

salt and pepper
1 × 10ml spoon/1 dessertspoon
  mixed dried herbs
juice of ½ lemon
2 × 15ml spoons/2 tablespoons
  beaten egg

GARNISH
lemon wedges
parsley sprigs

Make a cut down the centre of the entire length of each fish as for filletting. Loosen the flesh from the bone on each side of the cut, but do not detach it. Make the stuffing. Mix the cheese with the crumbs, mustard, seasoning, herbs, lemon juice and beaten egg.

Raise the two loose flaps of each fish and fill the pockets with the stuffing. Place the stuffed fish in a buttered oven-to-table baking dish, dot with the butter, and cover loosely with foil. Cook in a fairly hot oven, 190°C/375°F/Gas 5, for 20 – 30 minutes. Garnish with lemon wedges and parsley sprigs.

COD FILLETS IN BEER BATTER

Serves 4

350g/12 oz plain flour
1 × 15ml spoon/1 tablespoon
  vegetable oil
salt and pepper
250ml/8 fl oz light beer

150ml/¼ pint water
2 egg whites
900g/2 lb skinned cod fillets,
  cut into serving portions
oil *or* fat for deep frying

Mix 225g/8 oz flour with the oil, salt, pepper, beer and water. Whisk well for 3 – 5 minutes, then leave to stand for at least 30 minutes. Before coating the fish, whisk the egg whites until stiff and fold into the batter.

Season the remaining flour with salt and pepper, and roll each portion of fish in it, shaking off any excess. Dip immediately into the batter, and fry the fish in deep fat until golden-brown. Drain and serve immediately.

TROUT WITH ALMONDS

Serves 4

100g/4 oz butter
4 trout
salt and pepper
juice of ½ lemon

50g/2 oz flaked almonds
150ml/¼ pint double cream
3 egg yolks
parsley sprigs

Melt the butter in a grill pan under medium heat. Lay the trout in the pan, season, and sprinkle with lemon juice. Grill for 5 minutes, then turn the fish. Sprinkle with most of the almonds, spread the rest at the side of the pan, and continue grilling for a further 3 – 5 minutes until the trout are tender and the almonds are browned. Drain, then put the almonds to one side.

Mix the cream with the yolks and put into a small pan with any juices from the grill pan. Heat gently, stirring well, until thickened; do not let the mixture boil.

Lay the trout on a serving dish, and spoon the cream sauce over them. Garnish with the reserved almonds and with sprigs of parsley.

MACKEREL WITH GOOSEBERRY SAUCE

Serves 4

flour for coating
salt and pepper
8 mackerel fillets
50g/2 oz butter
juice of 1 lemon
25g/1 oz parsley, chopped

SAUCE
400g/14 oz gooseberries
50ml/2 fl oz dry still cider
25g/1 oz butter
1 × 15ml spoon/1 tablespoon
    caster sugar

Make the sauce first. Poach the gooseberries in the cider and butter until tender. Sieve to make a smooth purée, then add the sugar.

Meanwhile, season the flour with salt and pepper. Dip the fish fillets in the flour. Heat the butter in a frying pan and fry the fillets gently for 5 - 7 minutes, turning once. Remove them, arrange on a serving plate and keep hot. Reserve the butter in the pan.

Heat the gooseberry sauce in a saucepan and keep hot. Add the remaining butter to the pan, and heat until light brown. Add the lemon juice and chopped parsley, and pour this over the fish. Serve the gooseberry sauce separately.

INDIVIDUAL FISH PIES

Serves 4

50g/2 oz butter
2 small onions, chopped
50g/2 oz flour
600ml/1 pint milk
100g/4 oz Cheddar cheese,
    grated

a good pinch of dry mustard
salt and pepper
550g/1¼ lb cooked white fish,
    flaked
675g/1½ lb mashed potato

Melt the butter in a pan and cook the onions until soft. Sprinkle with the flour, and cook for 1 minute. Gradually add the milk and bring to the boil, stirring all the time. Add the cheese, and season to taste with the mustard and salt and pepper. Stir the fish into the sauce, then spoon into four individual dishes.

Put the potato in a piping bag fitted with a star nozzle and, starting from the centre, pipe outwards to cover the pies. Place the dishes under a low grill and heat until golden-brown.

Serve with a side salad.

SWEET AND SOUR PRAWNS

Serves 4

225g/8 oz peeled prawns
1 × 15ml spoon/1 tablespoon
  medium-dry sherry
salt and pepper
2 × 15ml spoons/
  2 tablespoons oil
2 onions, cut into rings
2 green peppers, cut into rings
150ml/¼ pint chicken stock
225g/8 oz canned pineapple
  pieces

1 × 15ml spoon/1 tablespoon
  cornflour
2 × 15ml spoons/2 tablespoons
  soy sauce
150ml/¼ pint white wine
  vinegar
75g/3 oz sugar

GARNISH
unpeeled prawns

Marinate the prawns in the sherry for 30 minutes and season well. Heat the oil in a saucepan and fry the onions and peppers gently until tender. Add the stock, and drain. Add the pineapple, cover and cook for 3 – 5 minutes. Blend together the cornflour, soy sauce, vinegar and sugar, and add to the mixture. Stir until thickened, then add the prawns and cook for 1 minute. Serve hot on a bed of boiled rice, and garnish with unpeeled prawns.

FISH PUDDING

Serves 4 – 5

100g/4 oz shredded suet
450g/1 lb white fish, filletted
  and finely chopped
50g/2 oz soft white
  breadcrumbs

parsley
salt and pepper
a few drops anchovy essence
150ml/¼ pint milk
2 eggs, lightly beaten

Mix together ths suet, fish, breadcrumbs, parsley, seasoning and anchovy essence. Lightly beat together the milk and eggs and stir into the mixture. Place in a greased 600ml/1 pint basin, cover with greased paper or foil, and steam gently for 1½ hours.

HERRINGS WITH MUSTARD SAUCE

Serves 4

4 herrings, heads removed and boned
2 × 5ml spoons/2 teaspoons lemon juice
salt and pepper
1 × 10ml spoon/1 dessertspoon dry mustard
2 egg yolks

50g/2 oz butter, cut into small pieces
2 × 15ml spoons/2 tablespoons double cream
1 × 15ml spoon/1 tablespoon chopped capers
1 × 15ml spoon/1 tablespoon chopped gherkin

Sprinkle the fish with lemon juice and season well. Grill, using moderate heat, for 3 – 5 minutes on each side. Keep hot.

Put the mustard and egg yolks in a basin and whisk over a pan of hot water until creamy. Whisk in the butter in small quantities. When the sauce thickens, remove from the heat and stir in the cream. Add the capers and gherkin, and season well. Serve hot with the herrings.

GOLDEN GRILLED COD

Serves 4

4 cod cutlets

TOPPING
25g/1 oz soft margarine
50g/2 oz mild Cheddar cheese, grated
2 × 15ml spoons/2 tablespoons milk

salt and pepper

GARNISH
grilled tomatoes
watercress sprigs

Place the fish in a greased shallow flameproof dish and grill under moderate heat for 2 – 3 minutes on one side only.

Meanwhile, prepare the topping. Cream together the margarine and cheese, then work in the milk, a few drops at a time, and season to taste. Turn the fish over, spread the topping on the uncooked side, and return to the grill. Reduce the heat slightly and cook for 10 – 12 minutes until the fish is cooked through and the topping is golden-brown. Serve garnished with grilled halved tomatoes and watercress sprigs.

Meat and Poultry

ROAST BEEF

a joint of beef suitable for roasting
salt and pepper

beef dripping (25g/1 oz per 450g/1 lb meat approx)

Weigh the meat to calculate the cooking time, allowing 15 minutes for each 450g/1 lb plus 15 minutes extra. Place the joint, fat side up, on a wire rack if available, in a shallow roasting tin. Season the meat, and rub or spread it with the dripping. Place the roasting tin in the oven and cook in a very hot oven, 230°C/450°F/Gas 8, reducing to fairly hot, 190°C/375°F/Gas 5, after 10 minutes. Transfer the cooked meat to a warmed serving dish, remove any string and secure with a metal skewer if necessary. Keep hot. Drain off the fat from the roasting tin and make a gravy from the sediment, if liked.

Serve with Yorkshire Puddings.

YORKSHIRE PUDDINGS

100g/4 oz plain flour
½ × 2.5ml spoon/¼ teaspoon salt

1 egg
300 ml/½ pint milk
lard

Sift the flour and salt into a bowl, make a well in the centre and add the egg. Stir in half the milk, gradually working the flour down from the sides. Beat vigorously until the mixture is smooth and bubbly. Stir in the rest of the milk.

Put small knobs of lard in individual deep patty tins. Place in a preheated hot oven, 220°C/425°F/Gas 7, until the fat is smoking hot. Half fill the tins with the batter and bake for at least 20 – 25 minutes, depending on the depth of the tins. The puddings will rise high above the tins, and will be almost hollow shells. Do not underbake or they will collapse when taken out of the oven.

19

RAISED VEAL, PORK AND EGG PIE

Serves 6

25g/1 oz plain flour
1½ × 5ml spoons/
    1½ teaspoons salt
½ × 2.5ml spoon/¼ teaspoon
    ground pepper
450g/1 lb pie veal, cut in to
    small pieces
450g/1 lb lean pork, cut into
    small pieces
3 hard-boiled eggs
2 × 15ml spoons/2 tablespoons
    water

beaten egg for glazing
150ml/¼ pint (approx)
    well-flavoured, cooled and
    jellied stock

HOT WATER CRUST
PASTRY
450g/1 lb plain flour
1 × 5ml spoon/1 teaspoon salt
175g/6 oz lard
250ml/8 fl oz milk *or* water

Prepare the pastry first. Sift the flour and salt into a warm bowl, make a well in the centre, and keep the bowl in a warm place. Meanwhile, heat together the lard and milk or water until boiling, then add them to the flour, mixing well with a wooden spoon until the pastry is cool enough to knead with the hands. Knead thoroughly, and mould as follows: Reserve one-quarter of the pastry for the lid and leave in the bowl in a warm place, covered with a greased polythene bag. Roll out the remainder to about 5mm/¼ inch thick, in a round or oval shape. Line a 20cm/8 inch pie mould with the pastry, taking care not to pull the pastry and making sure that the sides and base are of an even thickness. Leave to cool.

Meanwhile, season the flour with salt and pepper, and toss the pieces of meat in it. Put half the meat into the cooled pastry case and put in the whole eggs. Add the rest of the meat and the water. Roll out the pastry reserved for the lid, dampen the rim of the case, put on the lid, brush with beaten egg, and make a hole in the centre to allow steam to escape. Bake in a very hot oven, 230°C/450°F/Gas 8, for 15 minutes. Reduce the heat to very cool, 140°C/275°F/Gas 1, and continue cooking for 2½ hours. Remove the mould for the last 30 minutes of the cooking time and brush the top and sides of the pastry with beaten egg.

Heat the stock until melted and, when the pie is cooked, funnel it through the hole in the lid until the pie is full. Cool completely before serving.

LIVER AND POTATO CASSEROLE

Serves 4

50g/2 oz butter
225g/8 oz streaky bacon, rinds removed and chopped
350g/12 oz button onions
flour
salt and pepper
350g/12 oz lamb's liver, cubed
400g/14 oz canned tomatoes
1 × 15ml spoon/1 tablespoon Worcestershire sauce
100g/4 oz peas
175g/6 oz sweetcorn kernels
675g/1½ lb potatoes, sliced and parboiled
25g/1 oz butter, melted

Melt the butter in a pan, and fry the bacon and onions until the onions begin to soften. Season the flour with salt and pepper, then toss the liver in the flour and add to the bacon mixture. Cook until the liver is lightly browned. Add the tomatoes, Worcestershire sauce, peas and sweetcorn. Season to taste, heat to boiling point and simmer gently until the sauce begins to thicken. Transfer the liver and sauce to a casserole and layer the potato slices over the top. Brush with melted butter. Cook in a moderate oven, 180°C/350°F/Gas 4, for 45 minutes or until golden-brown.

BUBBLE AND SQUEAK

dripping *or* lard
thin slices of cooked meat
1 medium-sized onion, thinly sliced
cold mashed potatoes
cold, cooked green vegetables
salt and pepper
a dash of vinegar

Heat just enough dripping or lard in a frying pan to cover the bottom. Put in the meat, and fry quickly on both sides until lightly browned. Remove, and keep hot.

Fry the onion until lightly browned, adding a little more fat to the frying pan if necessary. Mix together the potatoes and green vegetables, season to taste, and add to the frying pan. Stir until thoroughly hot, then add a little vinegar. Allow to become slightly crusty on the bottom.

Turn the vegetables on to a warmed dish, place the meat on top, and serve.

FRIED PORK CHOPS
WITH PEACHES

Serves 6

6 pork chops
ground pepper
dried sage
1 × 15ml spoon/1 tablespoon
 oil
25g/1 oz butter
6 canned peach halves, drained
salt

1 × 15ml spoon/1 tablespoon
 plain flour
300ml/½ pint basic stock
 (see page 8)

GARNISH
mustard and cress

Sprinkle each chop with pepper and sage. Heat the oil in a frying pan. Add the chops, and fry until sealed and browned on the underside. Turn with a palette knife and continue to fry until the other side is browned. Reduce the heat and continue to fry, turning once or twice, until the meat is cooked through. The total frying time is 15 – 20 minutes, or longer for thick chops. Arrange on a warmed serving dish, sprinkle with salt and keep hot. Pour the fat from the pan, reserving the sediment. Melt the butter and add the peach halves. Fry gently until golden on both sides. Top each chop with a peach half, cut side down. Garnish with mustard and cress.

Stir the flour into the reserved sediment and cook. Gradually add the stock and stir until boiling. Season to taste. Serve the gravy separately in a sauce boat.

BEEF SALAD

Serves 4

1 Cos *or* Webbs lettuce
1 green pepper, thinly sliced
200g/7 oz sweetcorn kernels, drained
4 – 5 slices roast beef, cut into thin strips
100g/4 oz button mushrooms, each cut into four

DRESSING
2 × 15ml spoons/2 tablespoons sunflower oil
1 × 15ml spoon/1 tablespoon white wine vinegar
1 × 15ml spoon/1 tablespoon horseradish sauce
salt and pepper

GARNISH
bread croûtons

Tear the lettuce leaves into pieces, and put into a bowl. Add the green pepper, sweetcorn, roast beef and mushrooms.

Whisk together the dressing ingredients, pour on to the salad and mix well. Garnish with bread croûtons.

BOILED BACON WITH CIDER

any bacon joint suitable for
  boiling
cider
sugar
ginger root
4 cloves

6 – 8 black peppercorns
1 bay leaf
2 – 3 juniper berries

GARNISH
raspings
Demerara sugar

A bought or home-cured bacon joint will probably need soaking for
1 – 12 hours before cooking, depending on the saltiness of the meat.
Packaged and similar joints do not need soaking as a rule. They can be
put into a pan and covered with boiling water, then drained.

Weigh the joint and measure its thickness. Calculate the cooking time
according to the thickness of the joint. As a guide, allow 30 minutes for
each 450g/1 lb meat plus 30 minutes extra for any joint more than 10cm/
4 inches thick, eg cook a 900g/2 lb joint for 1½ hours. Do not undercook
the meat, but on no account cook it fast or it will shrink and be tough.

Scrape the underside and rind before boiling any bacon joint. Choose a
pan large enough to hold the meat comfortably with a little space to
spare, especially if boiling more than one joint at a time. Add enough
cold, fresh water and cider to cover the meat. Add the sugar and ginger
root. Tie the cloves in a square of muslin with the peppercorns, bay leaf
and juniper berries and add to the pan. Heat to simmering point, then
simmer steadily for the calculated time. Test for tenderness by piercing
the meat, near the bone if it has one, with a skewer.

Alternatively, shorten the cooking time by 15 minutes, and let the
meat lie in the hot cooking liquid, off the heat, for 30 minutes. This gives
an easier, firmer joint to carve.

Lift out the joint, pat dry, place it on a board and remove the rind. It
should come off easily, in one piece. Coat the skinned area thoroughly
with raspings, mixed with a little Demerara sugar. Serve hot or cold.

LANCASHIRE HOT POT

Serves 6

900g/2 lb potatoes
900g/2 lb middle neck of lamb
or mutton, cut into neat
cutlets
3 sheep's kidneys, sliced

1 large onion, sliced
salt and pepper
300ml/½ pint basic stock
(see page 8)
25g/1 oz lard *or* dripping

Slice half the potatoes, and cut the rest into chunks for the top of the casserole. Put a layer in the bottom of a greased, large, deep casserole. Arrange the cutlets on top, slightly overlapping each other, and cover with the kidneys and the onion. Season well. Arrange the remainder of the potatoes neatly on top, then pour in the hot stock. Heat the lard or dripping and brush it over the top layer of potatoes. Cover the casserole with a tight-fitting lid and cook in a moderate oven, 180°C/350°F/Gas 4, for about 2 hours or until the meat and potatoes are tender. Remove the lid, increase the oven temperature to hot, 220°C/425°F/Gas 7, and cook for another 20 minutes or until the top layer of potatoes are brown and crisp. Serve from the casserole.

TOAD-IN-THE-HOLE

Serves 4

75g/3 oz plain flour, sifted
1 × 5ml spoon/1 teaspoon salt
2 eggs
½ – 1 × 5ml spoon/

½ – 1 teaspoon prepared
mustard
300ml/½ pint milk
450g/1 lb chipolata sausages
100g/4 oz hard cheese, grated

Mix the flour and salt in a mixing bowl. Make a well in the centre and drop in the eggs and mustard. Gradually mix into a smooth batter, adding the milk, a little at a time. Put to one side.

Grill or fry the sausages until lightly brown. Meanwhile, grease four individual shallow tins, and heat in a hot oven, 220°C/425°F/Gas 7, for 10 minutes.

Whisk the batter until bubbly and stir in half the cheese. Mix well and pour in enough to half-fill each tin. Place the sausages in the centre and scatter over the remaining cheese. Bake for 30 minutes or until well risen and golden-brown. A skewer inserted in the batter will come out clean when it is cooked. Serve immediately, accompanied by a salad.

Toad-in-the-Hole (page 25)

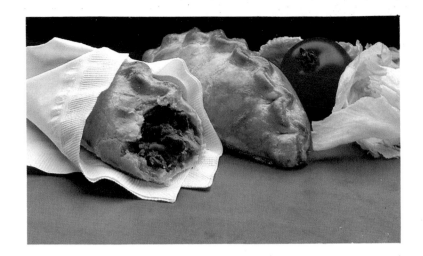

CORNISH PASTIES

Makes 8

100g/4 oz raw meat, minced
100g/4 oz potato, cut into
  1.25cm/½ inch cubes
50g/2 oz onion, finely chopped
dried mixed herbs

salt and pepper
2 × 15ml spoons/2 tablespoons
  gravy *or* water
350g/12 oz prepared shortcrust
  pastry
milk for glazing

Mix together the meat and potato. Add the onion with the herbs, seasoning and gravy or water. Roll out the pastry 5mm/¼ inch thick on a lightly floured surface, and cut it into eight 12.5cm/5 inch rounds. Divide the filling between the rounds, making a mound in the centre of each. Moisten the edges of the pastry, then lift them to meet over the filling. Pinch and flute the edges to seal. Prick the pasties with a fork and brush them with milk. Bake in a hot oven, 220°C/425°F/Gas 7, for 10 minutes, then reduce to moderate, 180°C/350°F/Gas 4, and bake for a further 50 minutes. Serve hot or cold.

Vegetables

MIXED VEGETABLE SALAD

Serves 4 – 6

3 large new potatoes
3 young turnips
½ bunch young carrots
225g/8 oz shelled peas
1 × 15ml spoon/1 tablespoon
 chopped parsley

1 × 5ml spoon/1 teaspoon
 chopped mint
150ml/¼ pint mayonnaise
salt and pepper
a pinch of paprika

Boil or steam the potatoes, turnips and carrots in their skins. Drain thoroughly, then peel and dice neatly. Boil or steam the peas. Add to the remaining vegetables with the parsley, mint, mayonnaise and seasoning, and mix well. Turn into a serving dish and sprinkle with a little paprika before serving.

TOMATO AND ONION PIE

Serves 4

450g/1 lb large onions, skinned
50g/2 oz butter
900g/2 lb tomatoes, skinned
 and sliced
salt and pepper

50g/2 oz Cheddar cheese,
 grated
50g/2 oz soft white
 breadcrumbs

Put the onions into a bowl, and cover with boiling water. Leave for 5 minutes, drain, dry thoroughly, and cut into slices. Melt half the butter in a pan and fry the onions until golden-brown. Place them in alternate layers with the tomatoes in a greased pie dish, sprinkle each layer lightly with salt and pepper and liberally with cheese and some of the breadcrumbs. Cover the whole with the remaining breadcrumbs and dot with the remaining butter. Cook in a fairly hot oven, 190°C/375°F/Gas 5, for 45 minutes.

CAULIFLOWER CHEESE

Serves 4

1 medium-sized firm
  cauliflower
2 × 15ml spoons/2 tablespoons
  butter *or* margarine
4 × 15ml spoons/4 tablespoons
  flour
250ml/8 fl oz milk

125g/5 oz grated Cheddar
  cheese
a pinch of dry mustard
a pinch of Cayenne pepper
salt and pepper
25g/1 oz fine dry white
  breadcrumbs

Put the cauliflower in a saucepan containing enough boiling salted water to half-cover it. Cover the pan, and cook gently for 20 – 30 minutes until tender. Drain well, reserving 150ml/¼ pint of the cooking water. Break the head carefully into sections, and place in a warmed greaseproof dish. Keep warm under greased greaseproof paper.

Melt the fat in a medium-sized pan, stir in the flour, and cook for 2 – 3 minutes, stirring all the time, without letting the flour colour. Mix together the milk and reserved cooking water, and gradually add to the pan, stirring all the time to prevent lumps forming. Bring the sauce to the boil, lower the heat and simmer until thickened. Remove from the heat, and stir in 100g/4 oz of the cheese, with the mustard and Cayenne pepper. Season to taste. Stir until the cheese is fully melted, then pour the sauce over the cauliflower. Mix the remaining cheese with the breadcrumbs, and sprinkle them on top. Place in a hot oven, 220°C/425°F/Gas 7, for 7 – 10 minutes, to brown the top. Serve at once.

Cauliflower Cheese (page 29)

MUSHROOM AND CUCUMBER SALAD

Serves 4

¼ Webbs lettuce, finely
  shredded
100g/4 oz button mushrooms,
  cut into quarters
½ cucumber, diced

DRESSING
4 × 15ml spoons/4 tablespoons
  mayonnaise

2 × 5ml spoons/2 teaspoons
  tomato ketchup
1 × 2.5ml spoon/½ teaspoon
  lemon juice

GARNISH
a pinch of paprika

Divide the lettuce between four salad bowls. Mix together the mushrooms and cucumber, and place on top of the lettuce.

Mix together thoroughly the mayonnaise, tomato ketchup and lemon juice and pour this over the mushrooms. Sprinkle with a little paprika.

Puddings and Desserts

RHUBARB CRUMBLE

Serves 6

550g/1¼ lb rhubarb, sliced
100g/4 oz brown sugar
50ml/2 fl oz water
grated rind of 1 lemon
75g/3 oz butter *or* margarine

175g/6 oz plain flour
75g/3 oz caster sugar
½ × 2.5ml spoon/¼ teaspoon
ground ginger

Cook the rhubarb in a covered pan until soft with the sugar, water and lemon rind. Fill a greased 1.2 litre/2 pint pie dish with the rhubarb. Rub the fat into the flour until it resembles fine breadcrumbs. Add the caster sugar and ginger and stir well, then sprinkle the mixture over the rhubarb, and press down lightly. Bake in a moderate oven, 180°C/350°F/ Gas 4, for 30 – 40 minutes until the crumble is golden-brown.

APPLE CHARLOTTE

Serves 5 – 6

450g/1 lb cooking apples,
  peeled, cored and sliced
grated rind and juice of 1
  lemon
100g/4 oz soft light brown
  sugar
a pinch of ground cinnamon

8 – 10 large slices white bread,
  5mm/¼ inch thick, crusts
  removed
50 – 75g/2 – 3 oz butter,
  melted
1 × 15ml spoon/1 tablespoon
  caster sugar

Simmer the apples, lemon rind and juice with the sugar and cinnamon until the apples soften to a thick purée. Leave to cool.

Dip one slice of bread in the butter. Cut it into a round to fit the bottom of a well greased 15cm/6 inch cake tin. Fill in any gaps with small pieces of bread. Dip the remaining bread slices in the butter.

Line the inside of the mould with six slices, touching one another. Fill the bread case with the cooled purée. Complete the case by fitting the top with more bread slices. Cover loosely with greased paper or foil, and bake in a moderate oven, 180°C/350°F/Gas 4, for 40 – 45 minutes. For serving, turn out and dredge with caster sugar.

Serve with bramble jelly and cream.

SPONGE PUDDING

Serves 6

175g/ 6 oz butter *or* margarine
175g/6 oz caster sugar
3 eggs
grated rind of ½ lemon
175g/6 oz plain flour

1 × 5 ml spoon/1 teaspoon
baking powder
2 × 15 ml spoons/2 tablespoons
golden syrup

Work together the fat and sugar until light and creamy. Beat in the eggs gradually, then add the lemon rind. Sift together the flour and baking powder and fold lightly into the mixture. Put the syrup into the base of a greased 900ml/1½ pint basin, then turn in the sponge mixture. Cover with greased paper or foil and steam for 1¼ – 1½ hours. Leave in the basin at room temperature for 3 – 5 minutes, then turn out.

Serve with warmed golden syrup.

LEMON PANCAKES

Makes 8

100g/4 oz plain flour, sifted
½ × 2.5ml spoon/¼ teaspoon
  salt
1 egg
2 × 5ml spoons/2 teaspoons
  caster sugar

300ml/½ pint milk
oil
lemon juice
extra caster sugar

Mix the flour and salt in a mixing bowl, make a well in the centre and add the egg and the sugar. Stir in half the milk, and beat vigorously until smooth and bubbly, then stir in the rest of the milk.

Heat a little oil in an omelet pan. Pour off any excess, as the pan should only be coated with a thin film of grease. Stir the batter and pour in 2 – 3 × 15ml spoons/2 – 3 tablespoons batter (just enough to cover the base of the pan thinly). Tilt and rotate the pan to ensure that the batter runs over the whole surface evenly. Cook over moderate heat for about 1 minute until the pancake is set and golden-brown underneath. Toss or turn the pancake with a palette knife, and cook the second side for about 30 seconds until golden. Slide out on to sugared paper, sprinkle with lemon juice, roll up and sprinkle with extra caster sugar. Repeat this process until all the batter has been used, greasing the pan when necessary.

Serve the pancakes accompanied by lemon wedges.

SUMMER PUDDING

Serves 6 – 8

900g/2 lb soft red fruit, eg
  black and red currants,
  blackberries, raspberries and
  bilberries
100 – 175g/4 – 6 oz caster
  sugar

a strip of lemon rind
8 – 10 slices day-old white
  bread (5mm/¼ inch thick),
  crusts removed

Put the fruit into a bowl with sugar to taste and the lemon rind, and leave overnight. Turn the fruit and sugar into a pan, discarding the lemon rind, and simmer for 2 – 3 minutes until very lightly cooked. Remove from the heat.

Cut a circle from one slice of bread to fit the bottom of a 1.5 litre/2½ pint pudding basin. Line the base and sides of the basin with bread, leaving no spaces. Fill in any gaps with small pieces of bread. Fill with the fruit and any juice it has made while cooking. Cover with bread slices. Place a flat plate and a 900g/2 lb weight on top, and leave overnight, or longer if refrigerated.

Served turned out, with chilled whipped cream.

Queen of Puddings (page 36)

QUEEN OF PUDDINGS

Serves 4

75g/3 oz soft white
  breadcrumbs
450ml/¾ pint milk
25g/1 oz butter
2 × 5ml spoons/2 teaspoons
  grated lemon rind

75g/3 oz caster sugar
2 eggs, separated
2 × 15ml spoons/2 tablespoons
  red jam

Dry the breadcrumbs slightly by placing them in a cool oven for a few moments. Warm the milk with the butter and lemon rind to approximately 65°C/149°F; do not let it come near the boil. Stir 25g/1 oz of the sugar into the yolks, then pour the warmed milk over the yolks, and stir in well. Add the crumbs and mix thoroughly. Pour the custard mixture into a greased 900ml/1½ pint pie dish and leave to stand for 30 minutes. Bake in a warm oven, 160°C/325°F/Gas 3, for 40 – 45 minutes until the pudding is lightly set.

Remove the pudding from the oven and reduce the temperature to very cool, 120°C/250°F/Gas ½. Warm the jam and spread it over the pudding. Whisk the egg whites until stiff, add half the remaining sugar and whisk again. Fold in the remaining sugar, then spoon the meringue over the pudding. Return to the oven for 40 – 45 minutes or until the meringue is set.

RASPBERRY FOOL

Serves 6

675g/1½ lb raspberries
sugar
600ml/1 pint double cream

DECORATION
fresh raspberries *or* whipped
  cream

Rub the raspberries through a sieve, then sweeten to taste, and leave to cool. Whip the cream until it holds its shape, then fold into the fruit purée. Turn into a serving bowl and chill before serving. Decorate with fresh raspberries or whipped cream.

APPLE FRITTERS

Serves 4

450g/1 lb apples, peeled and
  cored and cut into slices
lemon juice
100g/4 oz plain flour, sifted
½ × 2.5ml spoon/¼ teaspoon
  salt

1 × 15 ml spoon/1 tablespoon
  vegetable oil
150ml/¼ pint water
2 egg whites
caster sugar

Dry the fruit well, then put into water containing a little lemon juice until
needed.

Meanwhile, mix the flour with the salt, oil and some of the liquid, then
beat well until smooth. Stir in the rest of the liquid. Just before using,
whisk the egg whites until stiff and fold into the batter.

Drain the fruit well, then dry with soft kitchen paper. Coat with the
batter and fry, turning once, until crisp and golden. Serve hot, sprinkled
with caster sugar.

ORANGE SOUFFLÉ

Serves 4

2 oranges
75g/3 oz caster sugar
300ml/½ pint milk
75g/3 oz butter

50g/2 oz plain flour
4 eggs, separated
icing sugar

Finely grate the rind of both oranges. Squeeze the juice of one and put to
one side. Add the sugar and grated rind to the milk, heat gently to boiling
point, then turn off the heat. Leave to infuse for 5 – 7 minutes.

Melt the butter in a saucepan, stir in the flour and cook slowly for 2
minutes, without allowing the flour to colour; stir all the time. Add the
flavoured milk gradually, stirring constantly, and beat until smooth.
Bring the sauce to the boil and add the reserved orange juice. Remove
from the heat. Add the yolks to the sauce, one by one, beating well
together. Whisk the whites until fairly stiff. Stir 1 × 15 ml spoon/
1 tablespoon into the sauce, then fold in the remainder. Turn at once into
a buttered 1.2 litre/2 pint soufflé dish and bake in a preheated fairly hot
oven, 190°C/375°F/Gas 5, for about 35 – 40 minutes until risen and
browned. Sprinkle with a little icing sugar, and serve at once.

Above: Orange Soufflé (page 37)
Below: Raspberry Fool (page 36)

CHRISTMAS PUDDING

225g/8 oz plain flour
a pinch of salt
1 × 5ml spoon/1 teaspoon
   ground ginger
1 × 5ml spoon/1 teaspoon
   mixed spice
1 × 5ml spoon/1 teaspoon
   grated nutmeg
50g/2 oz chopped blanched
   almonds
450g/1 lb soft light *or* dark
   brown sugar
275g/10 oz shredded suet

275g/10 oz sultanas
275g/10 oz currants
225g/8 oz seedless raisins
225g/8 oz cut mixed peel
200g/7 oz stale white
   breadcrumbs
6 eggs
75ml/3 fl oz stout
juice of 1 orange
50ml/2 fl oz brandy *or* to taste
150 – 300ml/
   ¼ – ½ pint milk

Sift together the flour, salt, ginger, mixed spice and nutmeg into a mixing bowl. Add the almonds, sugar, suet, sultanas, currants, raisins, peel and breadcrumbs. Beat together the eggs, stout, orange juice, brandy, and 150ml/¼ pint milk. Stir this into the dry ingredients, adding more milk if required, to give a soft dropping consistency. Put the mixture into four 600ml/1 pint prepared basins, cover with greased paper or foil, and a floured cloth. Put into deep boiling water and boil steadily for 6 – 7 hours, or half steam for the same length of time.

Baking

MADEIRA CAKE

175g/6 oz butter *or* margarine
175g/6 oz caster sugar
4 eggs, beaten
225g/8 oz plain flour
2 × 5ml spoons/2 teaspoons
  baking powder

a pinch of salt
grated rind of 1 lemon
caster sugar for dredging
2 thin slices candied *or* glacé
  citron peel

Cream together the fat and sugar until light and fluffy. Add the eggs gradually to the creamed mixture, beating well after each addition. Sift together the flour, baking powder and salt, and fold into the creamed mixture. Mix in the lemon rind. Mix well. Turn into a greased and lined 15cm/6 inch cake tin and dredge the top with caster sugar. Bake in a moderate oven, 180°C/350°F/Gas 4, for 20 minutes, then lay the slices of peel on top. Bake for a further 45 – 50 minutes.

SHORTBREAD

100g/4 oz plain flour
½ × 2.5ml spoon/¼ teaspoon
  salt
50g/2 oz rice flour, ground rice
  or semolina

50g/2 oz caster sugar
100g/4 oz butter

Mix together all the dry ingredients. Rub in the butter until the mixture binds together to a paste. Shape into a large round about 1.25cm/½ inch thick. Pinch up the edges to decorate. Place on an upturned greased baking sheet, and prick with a fork. Bake in a moderate oven, 180°C/350°F/Gas 4, for 40 – 45 minutes. Cut into eight wedges while still warm.

MINCE PIES

Makes 12

450g/1 lb prepared flaky,
  rough puff *or* puff pastry
225g/8 oz mincemeat

25g/1 oz caster *or* icing sugar
  for dredging

Roll out the pastry 2.5mm/⅛ inch thick on a lightly floured surface, and use just over half to line twelve 7.5cm/3 inch patty tins. Cut out 12 lids from the rest of the pastry. Place a spoonful of mincemeat in each pastry case. Dampen the edges of the cases and cover with the pastry lids. Seal the edges well, brush the tops with water, and dredge with the sugar. Make two small cuts in the top of each pie, and bake in a very hot oven, 230°C/450°F/Gas 8, for 15 – 20 minutes or until golden-brown.

DROPPED SCONES

225g/8 oz plain flour
1 × 5ml spoon/1 teaspoon salt
25g/1 oz caster sugar
1 × 10ml spoon/1 dessertspoon
  cream of tartar

1 × 5ml spoon/1 teaspoon
  bicarbonate of soda
1 egg
150ml/¼ pint milk (approx)

Sift together the dry ingredients three times. Add the egg and milk gradually and mix to a smooth thick batter. Heat a lightly greased griddle or a very thick frying pan. Drop dessertspoonfuls of the mixture on to the griddle or pan. Tiny bubbles will appear and when these burst, turn the scones over, using a palette knife. Cook the underside until golden-brown, then cool the scones in a clean tea-towel on a rack. The scones will take about 3 minutes to cook on the first side and about 2 minutes after turning.

Above: Mince Pies (page 41)
Below: Dropped Scones (page 41)

RASPBERRY BUNS

Makes 12 – 14

225g/8 oz self-raising flour
½ × 2.5ml spoon/¼ teaspoon
    salt
75g/3 oz margarine
75g/3 oz sugar
milk

1 egg, beaten
4 – 5 × 15ml spoons/4 – 5
    tablespoons raspberry jam
egg *or* milk
caster sugar

Sift or mix together the flour and salt. Cut the margarine into small pieces in the flour, and rub in until the mixture resembles fine breadcrumbs. Stir in the sugar. Add enough milk to the egg to make up to 150ml/¼ pint. Add the liquid to the dry ingredients, and mix with a fork to a stiff consistency. This produces a sticky mixture which supports the fork. Divide into 12 – 14 balls, and make a deep dent in the centre of each ball. Drop 1 × 5ml spoon/1 teaspoon raspberry jam inside each, then close the mixture over the jam. Brush with egg or milk and sprinkle with sugar. Place on a well-greased baking sheet, space well apart, and bake in a fairly hot oven, 200°C/400°F/Gas 6, for 15 – 20 minutes until firm to the touch on the underside.

SAVOURY GRIDDLE SCONES

Makes 12

225g/8 oz self-raising flour
1 × 2.5ml spoon/½ teaspoon salt
1 × 2.5ml spoon/½ teaspoon mustard powder
50g/2 oz margarine
1 × 15ml spoon/1 tablespoon finely chopped parsley

1 × 2.5ml spoon/½ teaspoon dried mixed herbs
50g/2 oz streaky bacon, rinds removed, chopped and fried
5 × 15ml spoons/5 tablespoons (approx) milk

Sift together the flour, salt and mustard into a large bowl. Rub in the fat. Stir in the parsley, mixed herbs and bacon, and mix to a soft dough with the milk. Divide in half, and roll out each half on a floured surface into a round about 6mm/¼ inch thick. Cut each round into six even triangles.

Heat a lightly greased griddle, and cook the scones, four at a time, for 3 – 4 minutes on each side. Turn them with a palette knife when browned on the first side. Fold in a clean tea-towel until all are cooked. Serve warm, with butter.

CHEESE SCONES

Makes 10 – 12

225g/8 oz plain flour
½ × 2.5ml spoon/¼ teaspoon salt
50g/2 oz butter *or* margarine

4 × 5ml spoons/4 teaspoons backing powder
75g/3 oz grated cheese
150ml/¼ pint fresh milk

Sift together the flour and salt into a large bowl. Rub in the fat. Sift in the dry baking powder, add the cheese, milk, and mix well. Add the milk, and mix lightly to form a soft spongy dough. Knead very lightly until smooth. Rool out on a floured surface to 1.25 – 2.5cm/½ – 1 inch thickness, and cut into rounds using a 5cm/2 inch cutter. Re-roll the trimmings, and re-cut. Place the scones on a greased backing sheet and brush the tops with beaten egg. Bake in a hot oven, 220°C/425°F/Gas 7, for 7 – 10 minutes until well risen and golden-brown. Cool on a wire rack.

FLAPJACKS

100g/4 oz margarine
1 × 15ml spoon/1 tablespoon
    golden syrup
100g/4 oz sugar

50g/2 oz rolled oats
50g/2 oz self-raising flour
75g/3 oz crushed cornflakes

Mix together the margarine and syrup very gently. Mix the dry ingredients, pour on the margarine mixture, and mix well. Press into a greased Swiss Roll tin, and bake in a fairly hot oven, 190°C/375°F/Gas 5, for 20 minutes or until firm. Cut into fingers while warm, and leave in the tin to cool.

GINGERBREAD

225g/8 oz plain flour
½ × 2.5ml spoon/¼ teaspoon
    salt
2 – 3 × 5ml spoons/2 – 3
    teaspoons ground ginger
1 × 2.5ml spoon/½ teaspoon
    bicarbonate of soda

50 – 100g/2 – 4 oz lard
50g/2 oz brown sugar
100g/4 oz golden syrup *or* black
    treacle (or a mixture)
milk
1 egg, beaten

Sift together the flour, salt, ginger and bicarbonate of soda into a bowl. Warm the fat, sugar and syrup in a saucepan until the fat has melted. Do not allow the mixture to become hot. Add enough milk to the egg to make up to 150ml/¼ pint. Add the melted mixture to the dry ingredients with the beaten egg and milk. Stir thoroughly; the mixture should run easily off the spoon. Pour into a greased and lined 15cm/6 inch square tin and bake in a warm oven, 160°C/325°F/Gas 3, for 1¼ – 1½ hours until firm to the touch.

Oatmeal Biscuits *and* Flapjacks (page 45)

OATMEAL BISCUITS

100g/4 oz medium oatmeal
100g/4 oz self-raising flour
1 × 2.5ml spoon/½ teaspoon
    salt
a pinch of sugar

100g/4 oz butter *or* margarine
2 × 15ml spoons/2 tablespoons
    beaten egg
2 × 15ml spoons/2 tablespoons
    water

Mix all the dry ingredients together and rub in the fat. Mix the egg with
the water and use this to bind the dry ingredients together into a stiff
paste. Roll out on a lightly floured surface to just under 1.25cm/½ inch
thick. Cut into rounds with a 5cm/2 inch cutter. Prick the surface of the
biscuits with a fork and place them on a greased baking sheet. Bake in a
moderate oven, 180°C/350°F/Gas 4, for 15 – 20 minutes.